How to live the Jesus Life

How to live the Jesus Life

LE ROY DUGAN

DIMENSION BOOKS
BETHANY FELLOWSHIP, INC.
Minneapolis, Minn. 55438

This is a revision of a book previously
published under the title,
Youth's Exciting Possibilities.

ISBN 0-87123-660-5

DIMENSION BOOKS
are published by
Bethany Fellowship, Inc.
6820 Auto Club Road
Minneapolis, Minnesota 55438

Printed in the United States of America

Contents

Preface

The Man Jesus is on the move! Marching with Him across America are battalions of young people who are tired of living without a reason and afraid of dying without a cause. Most of all, they are determined to abandon sin and line up with God.

The series of short chapters which make up this little guidebook was written with the view of giving intensely practical aid to this intense generation.

These pages are addressed to those kids who have at least a spark of spiritual interest smoldering somewhere inside. They don't attempt to get at the bunch that doesn't feel any God-reach within.

Such a job I leave to others for the moment.

For a good number of years I have been privileged to work with youth. In a Bible institute, in summer camps, and while chaplain of a Christian high school, great numbers of teens have confided their hangups. From these varied stories I drew one simple conclusion: There is an appalling need for sound instruction on how to live the Jesus Life.

This book is positive. It is about realistic, workable, livable Christianity. It just might help you. Give it a try.

Introductory Chapter

A Scream for Help

For a long time I have been convinced that many Christian workers are living in an old-fashioned Fool's Paradise. I am *positive* that many preachers are.

Too often adult Christians refuse to face reality! They pet and fondle their illusions like an old maid caters to a cat. In their private little spiritual dream world, the coarse and ugly side of life is confined to reports in the daily papers. They are generally very reluctant to admit that anything sordid or sadistic could ever grip the nice young people who are under their personal jurisdiction. To them, rottenness is often a reality *in the abstract*, but never in the concrete.

Thank God, some of the naïveté is evaporating. But for the most part the smog of unreality is still very much with us.

It seems to me an enormous injustice is being done to our youth because of this attitude.

Christian workers are supposed to be people with the answers. They, of all people on the earth, are the carriers of solutions. But no problem is ever solved until it is *faced right, labeled right,* dragged to the light, and washed clear in the blood of Jesus. Note please: It has to be *faced first.*

Oh, how we would howl with righteous rage if one of our youngsters went to the physician in protracted pain and came home still in agony, plastered with band-aids as his only token of treatment!

How much more should we shriek at the idea of ladling out bland spiritual tonics to young hearts tormented by secret crimes and torn with personal civil wars.

It simply isn't fair to tell the kids, "Read your Bible, pray, and come to church," and let it go at that.

There is a lot more to it. They know it. God knows it. The devil knows it. Kids have problems—deep, strongly felt, and excruciating. And they spawn and multiply in the darkness of ignorance, pretense, and fear of exposure. Somebody with a heart jammed with love has got to help them spit it all out and spread it, piece by ugly piece, before the white light of Jesus' presence.

I slogged down the rugged road to perdition for years. No one ever got around to pointing a loving finger at me to call me the low-down sinner that I knew I was. Result: pretense—and pain. Church on Sunday (since my mother wouldn't let me avoid it) and garbage on Monday.

We are literally surrounded by a whole growing generation immersed in every imaginable type of evil. The only successful counter is a big, strong, honest God, who looks people squarely in the eye, tells exactly what He sees, and comes to grips with the *particular* problems that plague their daily existence.

God is the ultimate Realist. I am delighted that He is not like He is often described by some of His friends—a kind of sloppy, celestial sentimentalist pouring platitudes down through some kind of shapeless pipe in a kind effort to cover up what my conscience tells me has to be killed.

Today's crowd of turbulent, strong-feeling, experience-conscious young fellows and girls is making a lot of noise. Much of it is a *scream for help.* Come on, Mr. and Mrs. Middle-aged-Bible-Believer, get out of the fog, swallow hard, and HELP.

Part One

YOU CAN BE RESCUED

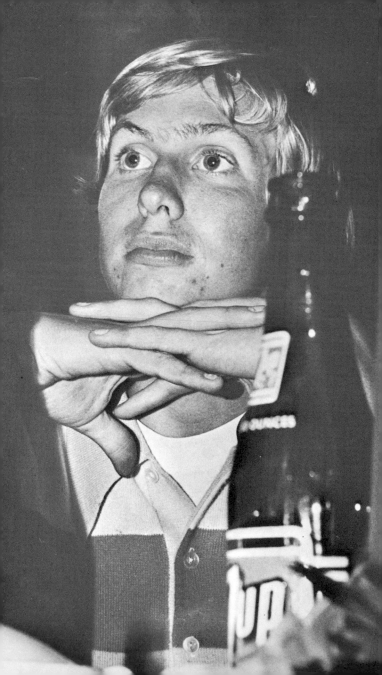

2

What Do You Really Need?

A soft and effeminate Savior is definitely not sufficient for this day and hour. We do not need a midget Jesus. We need a giant Jesus.

Bruce Barton wrote a book years ago, called *The Man Nobody Knows*. In most respects he missed the point by a wide margin, but in one way he hit the proverbial nail right on the noggin. He recalled that in his own Sunday school days the teacher told him every week, "You must love Jesus." Having absorbed that little commandment, his eyes turned to the painting of Jesus hanging on the wall. It showed a pale, flabby, sad man. Advice or no advice, he drew a solid, sensible little-boy conclusion, "Jesus is something for girls—sissified!" The artist had succeeded in making the Man into a mouse. What a tragic twist!

The real Jesus is God in human form. The real Jesus is masculine and mighty. The real Jesus offers all you really need. Not all you *want*, but all you *need*. There is an ocean of difference between the two. When my oldest boy was a child, he often approached me with a favorite pitch, "I *need* a nickel." What he *intended* was, "I *want* a nickel, but he had not yet learned to distinguish between the two ideas.

This leaves us with the question, What *do* you really need?

You Need a Pardon

When even a small child disobeys, he craves forgiveness. The need for pardon comes as standard equipment with each human being, and we are all aware of it at an early age.

When I was a youngster I was playing in a sandpile with a friend of mine. We were just outside his mother's kitchen window, and he was giving her a lot of lip for a long time. Finally, overwhelmed with a sense of guilt, he rushed to the open window and choked out, "I'm sorry." The passion for pardon was satisfied.

What that little fellow experienced is essentially what every mortal needs.

Once, at an outdoor carnival a few years back a nineteen-year-old was confronted on the subject of Jesus. He agreed to talk over his needs with a street preacher. As his sordid story poured out, he not only reviewed his personal sins but also confessed that for years he had wanted to talk to a minister about the condition of his soul. In spite of a life of muggings, robbery and thorough depravity, the longing for pardon was burning inside him.

This is true for both rebel and Christian.

If anything whatever mars the love relationship between a man and his God, the yearning begins to surface.

You Need Personal Love

One evening as I was putting my two-year-old son to bed, I re-learned something which every good mother already knows. I drew the shades, turned out the light, and plopped him unceremoniously into his crib. He immediately began to cry. My wife said to me, "Pick him up and hug him a minute, and he will be all right." I tried it. The result was perfect. He soon fell asleep.

I know that infant son of mine could not have explained it psychologically or scientifically, but within him was a God-given appetite for love.

There are numberless young people convinced they are outsiders because they find no genuine personal love expressed toward them. (Maybe you are among them.)

They become bitter, loud, and rebellious because they feel cheated. In such a state of mind they readily turn to any individual who seems to like them.

The results are often tragic.

What intensifies the tragedy is the fact that there is a wealth of personal love always available but not being used. Jesus himself offers the personal affection every person craves!

There is great need for understanding right at this point. Love is a delightful idea, a legitimate necessity. But it is also a badly misunderstood commodity. Love, Jesus style, is not primarily emotional. Simply stated, it is "a choice to act in the best interests of someone else." Sometimes it shows by affection, sometimes by discipline, sometimes by direct advice, but always with selfless intentions. Love is a determination to do the person next to us some genuine good. Love is an attitude God has toward you because He *chooses* to, and actions toward you because He deliberately desires the best for your life. Love, therefore, is not so much good *feelings* as it is good *intentions* and good *actions*. And because it is not just an exotic series of sensations, it is lasting and practical in a way that feelings can never be.

One black night an ancient American jeep, steaming like a miniature locomotive, was laboring along a Mexican highway. A radiator hose had broken, water was jetting through the wound and the rest was boiling away at a furious rate. There was no way of making repairs. The only recourse was to add water. But soon there was none. Greatly discouraged, the driver stopped alongside the roadway to wait for the dawn. When it came he awoke, stepped from the ailing vehicle and discovered that he had spent the night a mere stone's throw from a very deep well of water.

It is no exaggeration to assert that a huge crowd has come to a frustrated halt in the darkness of this world without yet discovering that a real experience of Jesus' love is within calling distance.

You Need Purity

Many years ago a handsome young sailor dropped to his knees alongside his bed and prayed a simple heartfelt prayer, "God, I'm dirty on the inside, and I want to be clean." He was already convinced that he had been pardoned. He was assured that he was loved. But he also knew that he was not *pure*.

A great number of people have prayed that kind of prayer. The catch is that very few believe it can really be answered. I know of one man who *did* believe. His name was Paul. This is how he put it, "The Spirit has made me free from the law of sin." There can be no doubt about it whatever. Jesus came to purify as well as pardon. In another place the same man wrote, "Christ Jesus gave himself on our behalf that he might . . . *purify* for himself a people." The moral mess in your interior life can be set straight. The craving for self-satisfaction can be cured and displaced by an overruling desire to satisfy GOD.

You Need Purpose

The person who lives without enlisting in a cause never lives at all. We were all made for a *reason*, and we must live for a reason.

Some years ago there was an up-to-date teenager in Carolina. An old-fashioned Bible thumper had come to town to hold some meetings. He carried the quaint name of Mordecai Ham. The teenage fellow took a croney of his to the tent for the express purpose of ridiculing the outlandish man at the front. It was not long, however, until the tide began to turn against the conspirators. They found themselves gripping the crude bench with all hands while the Spirit of God raked their consciences and rattled their brains. Ham's rousing sermon concluded with a very blunt appeal for action: "Come on up here and give yourselves to the Lord!"

The two fellows did just that. One of them was named Billy Graham. His biographer later wrote, "After that night his daily life became a daily adventure." He had not only found a Savior but a purpose for living.

You Need Personal Commanding

Someone came to a young acquaintance of his and told him he had found the Savior. The friend was very skeptical. He was invited to come and see for himself. He did. So overwhelmed was he by the man Jesus that he shouted, "You are the Son of God! You are the King!"

When he met the Christ, he knew at the same moment that he had met his Commander-in-Chief!

Billy Graham once reported that a survey among teenagers indicated one of the things they really wanted was *someone to command their lives.*

In the plan of God you have the amazing privilege of being under the personal jurisdiction of the greatest leader of all time.

Jesus is all you need. If you find yourself still managing some of your own affairs, it is simply because you have not taken Him for the *particular* need you have.

You need pardon, personal love, purity, purpose and personal commanding. Jesus functions as the supplier in each case. Unconditional surrender and confident faith open the door of entrance to Jesus in whatever capacity He is needed.

3

Has God Changed His Mind?

If we were gathered for a church service and had just finished the singing of the hymn which traditionally precedes the morning message, we might imagine hearing a loud, insistent knock on the door.

We would all instinctively turn around to look. (It takes almost nothing to distract us during church anyhow.) Wouldn't we be surprised if we saw an usher step back to admit a real live wierdo? Not the ordinary ding-aling commonly padding about the fringes of a modern American city, but a unique individual with the distinctive air of ancient history about him.

Picture him coming slowly up the aisle,

decked out in long robes. On his face is a very puzzled expression. A kind of reverent hush falls over the congregation.

The pastor steps back to allow the visitor to take his place at the front.

Very soon it becomes obvious that the strange, new person is unusual all right, but no odd-ball by any stretch of the imagination. His commanding presence surely deserves attention. He is Peter the apostle.

How he came is quickly overshadowed by the explanation of *why* he came.

"Friends. I am a confused man," he begins. "In my brain a question keeps hammering away: 'Has God changed his mind?' When I stood to my feet in Jerusalem long ago to explain God's way of salvation, His Spirit told me to say, 'Repent . . . and be converted that your sins may be blotted out.' But I have been going from meeting to meeting in your country, and I overhear Christians telling sinners, 'Only believe.' Why is it that God no longer insists that people must repent in order to be saved? Has God changed His mind?"

With that Peter's shoulders droop, the pained look still haunts his eyes, and he silently makes his exit.

Before we have a chance to recapture

our cherished cool, the door at the rear swings open again. Up the carpet strides another figure, turns on his heel, and raises his voice: "Listen. I have a question. 'Has God changed His mind?' I've been traveling this land of yours. I've eavesdropped on a thousand spiritual conversations. I keep hearing people being told, 'Just believe He died for you, and you will have eternal life.' But I'll never forget the day when God instructed me to write, 'The devils also believe and tremble' (James 2:19). But I have seen crowds of people assured they can enter God's Kingdom with the devil's faith. Can it possibly be that God has altered things that much?"

As he leaves we all somehow realize we have been listening to the apostle James.

By the time the third caller makes his entrance, we are really unnerved. These fellows have messed up our Sunday morning pretty thoroughly. We have had about enough.

But we are not off the hook yet.

Once more there are sounds of movement at the back. One more time a quaint stranger is moving toward the pulpit. He has a long white beard and is obviously very, very old. If the ushers had an impulse to throw him out, they stifled it out of consideration for his frailty.

Again the same insistent question comes. "Has God changed his mind?" says John. "I recall so well the words He caused me to pen, 'If any man love the world, the love of the Father is not in him' (1 John 2:15). But now I hear sinners being told that if they say they are saved and still love the world, they are simply to understand that they are 'worldly Christians.' But according to what the Spirit told me, nobody is ever both worldly *and* Christian, but worldly OR Christian."

Well, so much for our imaginary encounters. It's not too likely that either Peter, James, or John are going to be making any personal appearances in our serene sabbath services. But what they once wrote still stands.

No one ever became a Christian without first repenting.

Saving faith is faith in a PERSON, not just acknowledgment of facts.

Conversion is turning *away* from the world *to* Jesus.

There are many examples which could be cited of people who were convinced that God has not altered His thinking about what makes a Christian. One such example is Paul.

It's an exciting story. A fiery Pharisee rushes up the road to Damascus. He is at white heat, bristling with anger. Armed with official papers authorizing him to wipe out the Jesus people, he looks like a hungry hound on the heels of its prey. Suddenly something happens. He is blinded by a light and stunned by a voice! Now notice carefully how he became a Christian. It is all summed up in two questions he asked:

"WHO are you Lord?"
"WHAT do you want me to do?"

Paul had to ask the first question to be certain of the identity of the unseen speaker. But he did *not* have to make the second inquiry. He *could* have remained a rebel. There were other options open to him also: He might have told God he would pray about the matter when he got somewhere alone, or he could have insisted he already believed in the Messiah. (Without a doubt he assented to the fact that Jesus had existed and claimed to be the Savior.) But he did none of these things. As a matter of fact, the record does not even tell us that he "accepted Christ," or "asked Jesus into his heart," or "made his decision."

I am sure he "accepted," "asked," and "decided," but all such things are conspicuously absent from the account. Why?

Because none of them touched on the *real issue* in his life.

The issue with Paul, and every other sinner who ever lived is, Who will run my life?

For this reason Paul asked the question that made it possible for God to pour in eternal life: "What do you want me to do?"

It is not difficult to picture Paul standing up among the saints after this humbling encounter. Perhaps he would say something like, "When I started out from Jerusalem, I was my own boss. But along the road I submitted to Christ. And now JESUS IS MY BOSS."

In spite of everything people may have done to distort the message, God's real way of salvation remains intact. It is everlasting life by submission to Jesus Christ —submission expressed by genuine repentance and heartfelt faith in Him.

4

Let the Baptist Lead the Way!

Ninety-five percent of professing Christians are not really followers of Jesus. Somebody made that statement years ago. I do not know if it is true. Statistics like that are very difficult to measure. But, what if it is even approximately correct? How can there be so many individuals who believe the Bible to be true without being really converted?

Well, two things are certainly beyond question: Many who talk about Jesus are not actually His friends, and many who seem to become Christians desert Him very quickly.

It's a cinch these things were not present

at the time of the book of Acts. There is only one possible case of a false profession in the entire twenty-eight chapters of that great book.

So, it becomes painfully obvious that some of our American ideas about what it takes to get saved are very different from the Bible ideas on the subject.

As I thought these things over, I began to ask God just what the biblical steps to salvation are. I ended up looking carefully at a startling fellow called John, the Baptist.

I would like to suggest that you do the same for a few minutes.

According to the words of John, submitting to Jesus simmers down to three distinct steps:

Repent

When you open the New Testament you discover that the very first word of John's kick-off sermon was "repent." In plain, modern English this means, "Change your attitude about your sin." Matthew, chapter three, recounts the occasion on which this command was issued. This message was spoken six months before Jesus himself appeared publicly. And John told his hearers that the first imperative preparation for the coming of the Master was a genuine repentance.

Repentance is the starting place. All other steps to Christ become impossible without taking this one first. To attempt any other procedure is like a bride insisting she wants to be married but refusing to walk down the aisle to make the transaction. If she refuses the trip, she will never get the groom.

The Baptist is a masterful guide, especially at this point. The crowds jam in around him. He orders them to repent. Some are phonies. Others are very sincere. How will he know one brand from the other? I used to think that the more tears one shed, the more penitent he was. John knew better. He realized that a person who really means business about getting right with God will demonstrate it by two distinct symptoms. The first symptom is vertical, having to do with God himself. It is a wholehearted *confession of sin*! In other words, the guy who really has changed his attitude about his sins is eager to 'unload' to God. He wants to spill out the whole stinking record in the ear of the God he has so long abused.

Therefore, when the masses moved to the river bank to show their change of attitude, they aired their sins in confession to God.

The second symptom of repentance is *willingness to undo the past*, or straighten things out with fellow human beings. This is the horizontal evidence of the presence of a repentant attitude.

This is why John insisted that the throngs "produce fruit consistent with the repentance" they professed. (Williams translation)

The fellow who claims he wants to begin following Jesus, but doesn't want to apologize to those he has wronged, or return what he has stolen, is betraying himself. He has not yet repented.

Most of the things which go wrong in the lives of young people are related, directly or indirectly, to their parents. If there has been rebellion, it always begins at home. If there is disobedience, it started at home. If there is deception, it first showed at home. If there is sarcasm, it was first vented against Mother or Dad. In short, the first sinning was done against the two people whom God commanded kids to honor.

This means that the first batch of adjustments must be made with the authorities back home. Apologies must begin where wrongs were first done. The first money returned must go back to Mother's dresser or purse, or Dad's wallet.

Most basic of all, *the young person who claims to be serious about getting Jesus as Savior must be ready to make Mother and Dad his bosses.* Let us have no nonsense about this matter: Making Christ head of your spiritual life means making parents head of your natural life! This is not something invented by a hard-nosed preacher or a frustrated old man on the opposite side of the 'generation gap.' This arrangement was an invention of GOD. He wasn't kidding when He said, "Honor your father and your mother" and "Children, obey your parents."

Concentrate on Jesus

A number of men had joined up with John. Their idea was to prepare themselves for Jesus. They had repented. Then the critical day came. Suddenly the man of the wilderness pointed to the Man from heaven and said, "Behold the Lamb of God, which takes away the sins of the world." It was the signal to turn their total attention from themselves to the Savior. Until that moment it was imperative that they be largely preoccupied with themselves ...

in order to give themselves time to deal with their sins. But now Jesus had the spotlight.

What happened in that little incident was a lot like the story of the Asiatic monarch centuries before. She decided one day to take a trip through the length and breadth of her vast kingdom. So she commanded soldiers, artisans and laborers to go ahead to prepare the way for her coming. Where there was a valley they filled it and spanned it with a road. When they discovered boulders on the route, they removed them. Swamps were drained to make way for her majesty. In short, the realm was thoroughly prepared for the coming of the sovereign to be received by her subjects.

When Jesus walked down the path toward the followers of John, the same was true. The boulders, swamps, valleys and mountains of *attachment to sin* had been cleared away. The time had come to rivet their attention upon the only one qualified to remove their guilt.

Note carefully: Repentance, confession and restitution *cannot remove sin.* They are only the preparatory steps which *detach a man from his allegiance to it.*

Follow Jesus

Here was the grand climax—the finale

of finales. The Bible story simple states that the pupils of John deserted him and began to follow Jesus. Their first step of following was their first entrance into the kingdom of God.

What they did physically, all men must do spiritually. To those of us who no longer see Jesus in the flesh, this final act is to RECEIVE Jesus as Lord and Savior.

Many years ago a young person came to a pastor, looking like she was about to attend her own funeral. The reason for her gloom was simple, and she came right to the point, "I don't think I've really been saved." When asked what her spiritual experience had been, she explained that she had made a trip to an altar about four years previously. She stood at the front with several others for a few minutes and that was about all there was to it. No real meeting with Jesus. No intelligent transaction with God about her sin. Result: no assurance . . . no reality.

I suspect this has been the un-experience of great numbers of kids. Unhappy, unsatisfied, unrepentant, and very unsure. The cure is to follow the advice of John and step up into life.

5

Are You Thirsty?

A young American walked along a winding forest path in the mountains of northern Mexico. The rays of the sun stabbed through every opening in the canopy of leaves. The heat was almost unbearable. Perspiration poured off his body. Each step filled his mind with one persistent thought—*water*.

Never in his life had he been so thirsty!

Little lizards, wrinkled and dry, skittered over the hot, pebbly ground. Every stone was an oven and the sand like the surface of a stove. It seemed as if everything conspired to create thirst.

It was miles to the next village, and

the stream which flowed from the mountains after each occasional tropical downpour would certainly have dried up by now. Even if there were still a trickle of the cherished fluid farther along, it would be unthinkable to drink of it, for animals waded along its course and brought pollution with every step.

All of these things he knew quite well. But none of them slaked his thirst. The farther he trudged, the more intense it became. *Water*! Oh, for one swallow!

Then, suddenly, there it was—a clear, sparkling brook! At that moment it was the most beautiful sight imaginable. A gently laughing rivulet lazily moving through a miniature desert of sun-burnt stones. Before logic could gain control, the young man was on his stomach inhaling the delicious liquid.

Thirst had had its way.

Thirst must be quenched. It screams for satisfaction, and the longer it is forced to wait the louder it shrieks.

That fellow was thirsty enough to be led by his thirst instead of his head, and he was satisfied.

There are many young people who suffer from a thirst of a different sort—soul thirst. They are not getting anywhere because they are approaching the things of the Spirit *head* first instead of *thirst* first.

Now, that man with his face in the infested stream was making a mistake we must not make concerning spiritual things. He was getting a right craving satisfied in the wrong place. You may be doing the same. Maybe you've crammed your life full of useless extras, trying to make it more endurable. You must make up your mind to be finished with that foolishness.

Nobody was ever meant to be a complete person independently of Christ. That's why your mania for music and your frenzy for friends haven't done the trick. They are not supposed to. You were programmed for far better things. So, when the sound subsides and the crowd is gone, you still feel as hollow as before. Right?

Come on over to the River. His name is Jesus. Find out what to drink and how to drink.

At least three thirsts have their home inside you: 1) a thirst for pardon, 2) a thirst for purity, 3) a thirst for power. We talked about the first two in the first chapter of the book. Now, let's concentrate on the third. According to the seventh chapter of John, the Master once said, "Whoever is thirsty should come to me and drink. . . Whoever believes in me, streams of living water will pour out from his heart" (7:37).

Then He explained exactly what He meant: "Jesus said this about *the Spirit*, which those who believed in him were going to receive" (7:39). To make it still more clear, He told His followers later that they would be "*filled with power* when the Holy Spirit" came upon them (Acts 1:8).

This is terrific! Power to replace your weakness. Energy from God to give you what it takes to broadcast Christ to an antagonistic generation. If you are a Christian, this is precisely what you want. It's tailor-made for a person like you. Only one question remains, "How do you get what Jesus was talking about?"

Since it is true that everything spiritual which any Christian ever had, YOU can have, then present yourself as a candidate for the power of the Holy Spirit. Now, take three indispensable steps:

Renounce the Past

Face up to it. You have been drinking so long at the wrong fountains that you have actually become attached to them. Decide to put an end to that. You want one spirit, and one spirit only, to change your life—the Spirit Jesus offers. Repent of the junk that has accumulated like uncollected garbage. "If we confess our sins to God . . . he will forgive us our sins and make us clean from all our wrongdoing" (1 John 1:9).

Rejoice at the Prospect

There was once a whole group of men very much like you. They were long on talk and short on courage. They loved Christ but they feared men. Like all Jesus' followers since their day, they were in desperate need of a dose of divine dynamite. The Bible calls them apostles. Jesus once told them, "You must wait in the city until the power from above comes down upon you" (Luke 24:49). When they heard that promise, they got so excited they began to praise God. They were convinced the dull, defeated life they had been living was about to come to a spectacular halt, and a new kind of Christian life was going to begin. The marvel about the whole thing is this: They were so certain they were going to get God's power that they immediately started a welcome party—days before the Spirit actually came.

When you see that the Bible promises power for you also, begin to express your certainty by praising Him for what He's going to do.

Receive the Person

This is the simplest step of all because it is very much like something you did once before. To become a Christian, you received Christ as a person into your life. To become an empowered Christian, you deliberately receive the person of the Holy Spirit.

When you were a little kid your dad offered you a nickel. He said, "Take it, son." You reached out, grasped it, and it was yours. The transfer of five cents was complete—all for the taking. Then you grew up a little, and the moment arrived when your father knew you were ready for a bigger need. So he extended his hand once more; this time it held the keys to the car. You didn't need a special explanation of what to do. You had learned how to *take*, and now you knew how to respond.

God the Father gave you Jesus. You received Him. Now Jesus the Son offers you His other self—the Spirit. Receive *Him*.

If you have read this far, be encouraged. But don't stop now. Things are not likely to get better by themselves. If you are good and tired of your ineffectiveness, put this book down, get on your knees, and take the necessary steps to power.

Part Two
YOU CAN WIN

6

Six Suggestions for Spoiling Saints

(Advice whispered by the enemy into the ears of a young Christian)

A small, friendly (but invisible) underling of Satan slips into the room of a healthy young man one morning, pulls a chair alongside him as he reaches for his Bible, and begins to breathe the following sane-sounding advice into his ear:

"Why should you get up every morning to read the Bible and pray. Man, you can be a good Christian without missing all that sleep. Look at your Ma ... She's a Christian, and she sticks to the mattress till the last possible moment. And you know good and well there isn't one kid in ten in your Christian crowd that bothers with 'devotions' before their Wheaties. Be reasonable. It's obvious you don't have to part with your pillow early to be an acceptable saint. You can pray later in the day, and feel a lot sharper in the process."

There are sounds of an extended yawn, a closing Bible and squeaking bedspring sinking under the burden of a retreating believer. Then, silence . . . and a smile on the face of the whispering intruder.

Finally, the victim wakes with a start, checks his watch, and leaps from the bed. "Just got time for half a breakfast and a fast sprint to school." When he reaches for his books on the way to the front door, the small voice croaks again.

"Don't take that Testament to school today. Be sensible. The reason you are not getting anybody converted is that you wave that flag everywhere you go. That little book is a dead give-away. You gotta be more subtle."

The New Testament is lying on the hall table when the door slams behind the departing pair. Three minutes later a horn blasts, brakes squeal and a voice calls out, "Hey, Ned. Hop in. It's late. You'll never make it walking!"

Ned squeezes into the car with five other fellows. The air is thick with foul language. It's like sitting in a sewer. Jesus is ridiculed and his Father is profaned. It is time for a word from defense counsel, but before Ned has time to clear his constricted throat there is a soft suggestion from the accuser.

"You're too scared to witness, aren't you? Well, you should be. This is a rough bunch. Stick your neck out and one of them will step on it. Anyhow, they aren't interested in religion. If they were they wouldn't be talking like this, now would they? Keep mum until you get a better opportunity some other time."

The defense rests . . . out of sheer fear. They pull into the school parking lot and pile out. The little whispering expert is smiling again. It certainly has been a good day so far.

After the morning classes are over, Ned stuffs his books into the locker and is about to head for home when his eye falls on a brightly colored something on the floor. Curiosity carries him to it, and he picks it up. A book. One of those sleezy sex stories. A voice inside of him says "No," but the diminutive messenger from the outside says, "Go ahead. Read it. How can you understand the way sinners think if you don't even know what they read? You know, that's half the trouble with you, boy—you're so sheltered. You have isolated yourself from reality. You don't know how to cope with it anymore. No wonder you aren't reaching kids for Christ. Go on. Read!''

Our un-hero is late for dinner. One page had led to another, and another. He hadn't planned to read so much, but he'd gotten hooked. He doesn't enter into the table talk much. His mind is a maze of shabby pictures. His insides feel all messy.

By the time school is out he is pretty depressed. It's been a rough day: no prayer, no Testament, no testimony, no peace. He sure doesn't feel like going to Bible Club. What if they ask for testimonies? He'd either have to fake it or stare at the floor in silence.

The enemy's persistent representative is still alongside, waiting for the next opening. And here it comes:

"Hi, Ned. Been looking for you. A bunch of guys are getting up a game of touch on the old practice field. We need all we can get. Come on out."

The timing could not have been better. The perfect break. Right on cue the whisper comes through, "Here's your chance to get out of the dumps. It won't hurt to miss Club once. Fact is, it will probably do you a lot of good. A young fellow like you needs some exercise after sitting in class all day. Furthermore, you'll be a better witness out on that field, showing them a Christian is no sissy, than you would be going to a gospel meeting. Let's go."

Ned is really shot when he gets home for supper. He eats without words and goes upstairs to his room. Suddenly it hits him: "It's prayer meeting night. I'll have to hit the books right away so I'll have time to get ready." The prospect of going to church is like a shot in the arm. He can talk the whole day's mess over with the Lord and get it all cleared up.

Just then the phone rings. The little intruder is delighted to discover that on the other end of the phone is Eileen, the cutest girl in school. He tip-toes to the phone in time to hear her honeyed voice dripping over the wire. "Ned. Can you come down to Andy's? Lots of the bunch are here already. We're all going over to the Amusement Park at Princeton, and I want you to take me." She couldn't have had more effect if she had stabbed him. The only difference was that his blood was not running on the floor. It just began to accelerate from the pit of his stomach to his temples, and made it hard for him to swallow or breathe properly. It took only one brief admonition from the invisible one to tip the scales decisively: "Say yes, idiot! You've been wanting a date with her for months. And it is probably your chance to win her to the Lord."

He was going to say more, but it wasn't at all necessary. Ned had consented, and bolted out the front door before he was half through his third sentence.

It is very late when they drop him off in front of his house. He waves a limp good-bye and goes up to bed—tired, but not sleepy; home, but not happy.

Over in the corner is his close companion of the day. He is still small, still friendly, and supremely happy. He had offered six suggestions and spoiled a saint. He will be there in the morning to try again.

7

How To Master Temptations

A friend of mine once told me that he had only one problem in his Christian life—temptation.

He was, of course, correct. This IS the problem in the Christian life. And for this reason we must know how to handle it.

But, to use Mr. Nixon's phrase, "I want to make one thing perfectly clear." A person who is a Christian does not make a *practice* of sinning. What we are concerned with are inducements to wander temporarily from the right kind of life. People who still make a practice of sinning do not find temptation much of a problem. Temptation is to them what air is to a bird—the means by which they can keep living in the atmosphere they enjoy. Not so with the follower of Jesus. He knows temptation is like a sniper, bent on blasting him out of blessing.

Assuming, then, that you have joined up with Jesus and want to live the Jesus life, you may find some of the following suggestions helpful.

Keep Away from the Causes of Temptation

There is no doubt that much of the difficulty comes from unnecessary contact with tempting things. A young man may feel terribly drawn to the world's way. He cannot understand why. The solution is ridiculously simple: On his bookshelves are bawdy magazines and sex-sprinkled periodicals. He cultivates an appetite for questionable movies and suggestive television programs. Small wonder that this present world becomes such a magnet.

Avoiding unnecessary temptation may mean concelling some magazine subscriptions and turning off the tube. It may mean ditching certain types of music, smashing a lot of records, or dropping some old friends.

Whatever is necessary must be done.

If not, there is no point in expecting God to help you overcome temptation.

Adopt the Right Attitude
Toward Temptation

When unavoidable temptation begins to bug you, the Bible says, "Consider yourselves fortunate" (James 1:2). At first glance that sounds ridiculous and pointless. But it is neither. God never allows a temptation without a definite purpose in mind. It is one of the means He uses to allow you to build spiritual muscles.

There is a fanciful story of a weakling who drank a magic potion which affected his make-up in a marvelous way. Every time he was bumped or struck by someone else, he got stronger. It was so effective that he was soon transformed from Mr. Frail to Mr. Superman.

The Lord is after something like that in allowing His children to be battered by temptation.

Do Not Concentrate on Temptation

Concentrating on something invariably has the effect of making it appear more powerful than it is. Any young athlete will tell you that the longer he looks at the opponent across the football field the bigger he seems to get.

When you are being tempted about something, it is sometimes best not even to talk it over excessively in prayer, because rethinking the matter makes it seem more irresistible.

Then, too, some people talk to others so much about the bad times they are having that the effect is the same. It is right to take your temptations to God and to understanding friends. But constant rehashing of them will only make matters worse. Nowhere in the Word of God are we directed to concentrate on temptations.

Do Not Struggle with Temptation

We need to be cautious at this point. The Bible reminds us to resist, pray, and be on guard, but it never suggests we are big enough to win by ourselves.

Remember the story of the self-sufficient rabbit and the tar-baby? Well, in case your mother forgot to include it in your early education, I'll refresh your memory.

This particular rabbit came upon a tar figure on a stick, put up by a farmer as

a kind of scarecrow. When the black creature refused to engage in conversation, the
rodent felt insulted enough to whack him.
Of course he stuck fast. This made him
still madder, so he used another paw, and
another, until he was thoroughly entangled
in the sticky stuff and was finally unable
to move. The illustration may sound juve-
nile, but the lesson is unmistakable. Christians very often do the same thing with
their temptations. As long as a believer
wrestles with will power alone, he is certain
to lose the match.

Do Not Blame the Devil for Your Tempta-
tions

When this statement first found its way
into print, I received a letter from a lady
who said it confused her. You may feel
the same way. This confusion is understand-
able, and I appreciate the need for clarifica-
tion.

We are not suggesting that the devil
is not the original tempter. We do not imply
that temptation comes from God. All we
say is the devil does not personally pay
us a visit each time we sense the pull toward
sin. He is chief of God's enemies, but he
cannot be present in all places at all times.

It is highly unlikely that most of us will ever be confronted by Satan in that completely personal way. If we attribute every temptation to a special visit from the Prince of Darkness, the trial will look insurmountable. Further, pointing the finger at the devil shifts the responsibility for right choices away from ourselves, and suggests we are simple pawns of the enemy and not really TO BLAME for our actions.

It is much more accurate to describe temptation the way God does. He tells us, "A person is tempted when he is drawn away and trapped by his own desire." (James 1:14).

Overcome Each Temptation by Faith

The Book does not say, "The life that I now live I live by struggling, striving or straining." It says I live "*by faith.*"

Every brick the adversary throws can be deflected by one thing only: *faith* in Jesus. Nobody claims it is always easy, but we insist it is always *effective*. It works, because it's God's way of doing it.

I know it sounds too simple. Maybe that's why it is too seldom tried.

All right, what IS faith? It is *immediate confidence in Christ.* On the spot, when

the pressure to do the wrong thing is squeezing the breath out of you, throw yourself
on Jesus. Victory then is in His hands. The
outcome is sure!

8

Are You on the Offensive?

On December 7, 1941, our country suffered perhaps the greatest defeat in its history. The air and sea forces of imperial Japan descended upon three of our Pacific bases in a swift surprise attack. At Pearl Harbor five of our battleships and over 2500 of our men were suddenly put out of commission. When the attacking planes finally turned back to their carriers, they left behind them the flaming graveyard of a great part of United States fighting power. Ships of battle were swallowed in the sea; aircraft were consumed in fire; and men were hurled over the brink of eternity.

In one terrible blow, the greatest nation on earth had been knocked off its feet and forced into a defensive position.

Exactly five months later the tide began to turn. After just three more months American Marines went on the offensive and began the push that ended in total victory. The final triumph did not come for over three years, but it was the early change from *defensive* to *offensive* position that brought it to pass.

I'd like to suggest that the vast majority of Christian youth are living *on the defensive*, when they could be pushing on to victory.

Take a serious look at a defensive young Christian:

First: Watch him when temptation comes swinging by. He has to muster every particle of energy to fight it to a draw. Too often he simply surrenders. If he gives up he hates himself afterwards, but sees little hope for a more successful future.

Second: Watch him when the world baits him. He sees it. He hates it. He wants no part of it. It's the same system that did away with his Savior. But if he is living defensively, his armor is rusty and full of cracks, and before long the pollution of the 'modern' way of thinking has seeped through and stinks up his mind. He begins to agree with ideas he could never prove from the Bible. He starts justifying practices he once abhorred. His philosophy of life becomes a weird mixture of Holy Writ and hard rock.

Third: Note his response when his Lord comes by. Because Christ is within him, he experiences concern for the spiritual welfare of others. But he has been so busy fighting his own inward battles that he is in no shape to seriously join the struggle for the conversion of sinners.

Mind you, our friend gets very excited when he is part of a mammoth Jesus Rally. His enthusiasm is boundless when surrounded by cheering crowds listening to the currently popular folk groups. When another entertainer professes Christ, he thinks it's great. He will go half way around the world on a witnessing campaign—provided he is always surrounded by swarms of other likeminded kids.

Unfortunately, he still must live inside his own skin, on a one-to-one basis with God and other people. And here, where it is really at, he is still on the defensive.

In other words, the defensive Christian can, in a very real way, be part of the wonderful thing the Spirit of God is doing across the world—the rallies, the singing, and the mass evangelism—and still be a *personal flop*.

Incidentally, is this the way it is with you?

Is there any help for such a Christian? The answer is an emphatic "Yes." God has a way and a means of taking this kind of individual off the defensive and launched out in positive living.

His *way* is the cross. His *means* is the Holy Spirit.

The 'way of the cross' means the defeated Christian renounces and confesses all sin and gives himself to God with no strings attached—in a decisive, total self-giving. Having done this, he discovers God takes him in hand in a new way, and shows him His intention to destroy every fragment of the offering which did not originate in heaven. If this sounds too vague, perhaps an illustration will help.

Imagine you are a building contractor, and a carpenter comes and offers to build your next house. He promises to place himself at your disposal and build according to your specifications. So, you take him to the lumber yard (which you also own) and tell him that *all* the material which is to go in the structure *must* come from your own supplies. Furthermore, you make it clear that neither work nor materials which are not according to your exact plans can be accepted. Some weeks later you go to see the site. What a shock!

The structure before you can be called a house by only the broadest possible definition of the term. Everything is wrong. It is obviously a kind of three-dimensional scrap collection.

You call the carpenter at once.

He is discouraged and very much ashamed. "I got cut-rate material and had some left-over lumber of my own, and tried to combine it in order to save money. Then, too, along the way I got some design ideas which seemed pretty good at the time. I really didn't think it would look this bad. I've made such a mess of the whole job I don't know where to go from here."

At this point you take pity on the carpenter and offer him a proposition. "All right. I've got a wrecking crew available for situations like these. With your permission we'll raze this building. Any material you didn't get from me will go to the bonfire. Now, you'll get no pay for your faulty work to date, since you broke your contract. However, I want to give you another chance. You turn it all over to me. I'll tear it down, and you can begin again with proper supplies, if you will follow the original plans."

This is about what God wants you to do.

None of your sin-soaked talents, pride-bloated personal plans, or old habits are suitable materials for the construction of a new life. Therefore, to go God's way is to give everything over to Him for destruction. *That* is the way of the cross. You see, when Jesus died He was completing a kind of legal transaction—understood well by both God and the devil—which makes it lawful for Him to both destroy the ingredients in your former way of life and offer you a brand new one as well.

The question which remains is, "Will you give your whole self over to God for the destruction of everything which does not please Him?"

In the second place, we must examine God's *means*—the Holy Spirit. God's *way* presents the proposition to the Christian, but God's *means* can make it actually happen.

There are so many young people who have realized they are building shabby, unsatisfactory Christian lives. But they try to remedy the sad situation by repeated (and somewhat indefinable) reconsecrations. In other words, they have at least *tried* to cooperate with God's way. But usually nothing much changes. Many times the reason is that they have *failed to receive* God's Spirit who can make the promises of victory really come true!

Are you on the defensive? The tide can turn for you if you will follow God's way and personally *take* His Means.

9

Love Not the World!

"The Lord put the church in the world, and the devil put the world in the church!" a preacher shouted many years ago.

In one way he was completely right, but in another he was dead wrong.

There is no doubt that behind the scenes, the devil has been pulling some strings. But up on center stage it's the *church itself* which has been making love to the world.

But, wait a minute. It will do none of us any good to speak about the "church." That's far too vague. Sounds like another frontal assault on that mystical thing we call the "religious establishment," or "organized religion." Firing broadsides at the church has been a favorite recreation of both young and old for many a year, but it hasn't done much in the way of producing better followers of Jesus. And the reason is that the ammunition has been expended on the wrong target. If any constructive criticism is in order, then each individual Christian must first turn the muzzle upon himself. In the case of the subject now before us, this means we must first carefully examine *ourselves* individually concerning worldliness.

So, from this point onward let's look in the mirror. What do we see?

Well, the usual picture may be something like this: An ordinary young Christian with a set of standards drawn largely from his own particular religious environment. 1) I don't dance. 2) I don't smoke (either cancer sticks or pot). 3) I go only to 'G-rated' movies. 4) I keep away from booze. 5) I don't go 'too far' when I'm on a date.

Just a minute please. All these rules may be fine. But the fact of the matter is, any self-respecting pagan could subscribe to the same code. More than that, you can stick to that neat list of regulations and still be as worldly as the devil himself.

Now don't get all shook. Hear me out, please.

Let's start with a definition.

The word "world" is used about two hundred times in the New Testament. It simply means "this age, or present arrangement of things." Well, that sounds harmless enough. But let's move on. Next question:

How does God describe the *nature* of this world? Viewed through His eyes, what does it look like?

If we squeeze together the most important verses, we can come up with a compact one-sentence description. Here it is:

"The world is an arrangement of things which is evil, antagonistic to God and Christians, defiling, ruled by Satan, and destined for judgment day." *

Suddenly it no longer sounds so innocent, does it?

One more very important step must be taken. We have to discover what God says about our relationship to such a distorted thing.

---

*Galatians 1:4, John 7:7, James 1:27, John 14:30, Ephesians 2:2, John 16:8.

Again, compressing many Bible passages into one short statement will bring us a plain picture of the will of God. He says we have been delivered from the world and therefore are to deny it, refuse to conform to it, keep unspotted from it, be crucified to it, and be completely antagonistic to what it represents." *

Read through that sentence again. Does that describe your relationship to this present order of things?

Now let's get right to the core of the affair. According to the stated opinion of the ONE EXPERT on the subject—God—*worldliness is wrong relationship to the present arrangement of things in this planet.* Notice, please: a wrong *relationship.* It is essentially a matter of the heart. Worldliness lives in the heart, if it lives anywhere at all. We have been far too inclined to describe it in terms of *nouns*, like booze, drugs, dirty movies, and topless taverns. But God puts the emphasis on *verbs.* So He says, "If any man *love* the world," "*gain* the whole world," "*hate not* his own life in this present world," "*will be* a friend of the world," etc. These are verbs, verbs of attitude, which produce verbs of action.

---

* Galatians 1:4, Titus 2:12, Romans 12:2, James 1:27, Galatians 6:14, Hebrews 11:7, John 12:25.

But they all say essentially the same thing, "Don't get hung up on anything but God."

Now, if a girl keeps away from liquor but would be delighted to have a 'snort' if circumstances permitted, she is as worldly as the alcoholic in the gutter (but not as honest). If a "saintly" gal gasps at the sight of a micro-mini on someone else, but craves new clothes all the time, she may be far more worldly than the immodest maiden who jarred her sense of propriety. The young man who piously frowns at his school mates' beer consumption but cannot tear himself away from the 'tube' may be as bad off as the boozers. Those who wag their heads at the obvious overexposure decreed by today's dress designers are correct in assuming that many of the wearers are worldlings. But if the same critics are addicted to food, their problem is probably more acute than that of those they judge.

You see God is not as superficial in His analysis as we often are. That's why He doesn't stop with commands like, "love not gin," or "love not *Playboy*." He is more inclusive, more cutting. He plunges to the very center of the issues and insists, "Don't fasten your heart on anything less than myself!" To make your commitment to anything else is to be in wrong relationship to the world.

71

Before we finish, two more things need saying. The first is this: There is no such thing as a worldly Christian. If a Christian becomes worldly, he *ceases* being a Christian. Let me quote the Expert once more: "If any man love the world, the love of the Father is not in him" (1 John 2:15). The Bible describes the world, and defines Christians, but never gets the two mixed. You are either a child of the world or a child of the Father. You cannot be both at the same time. To put it bluntly, "There ain't no such animal as a worldly Christian."

The final question which we must ask is, "How can a Christian ever become a worldling again?"

The brief answer to this query is suggested by a statement made by the apostle James. He wrote, "Pure religion . . . is this . . . to keep oneself *unspotted* from the world" (James 1:27). It can happen by contact. Spots always occur that way. The Christian lives in a filthy moral environment. Dirt is all about him. The keeping power of God extends to the edge of our *necessary contact* with that dirt, but not one inch beyond! The moment a believer steps over that borderline, he has no promise of God's preserving presence. He loses cleansing contact with God when he establishes corrupting contact with this present order of things. But, tragically, that is not the end of the story. What starts as contact from *without* can soon be transformed to content *within*—and he has become a worldly hearted traitor to the same Jesus who once washed him clean.

The Christian who argues that what he toys with *externally* cannot damage him *internally* is a first-rate fool. What he fails to see is that with every "thing" of the world, there is always the "spirit" of the world (1 Cor. 2:12, Eph. 2:2).

You may mess around with something and then throw it aside when it begins to get a little boring (because eventually everything in this age loses its kick). But dumping the *thing* does not mean you have evicted the *spirit of the thing*. Maybe the thing cannot move into your heart, but the spirit of it certainly can. And *that* is the crux of worldliness!

Well, I've said enough. At the beginning of this chapter I suggested you look in the mirror. What have you seen in that glass?

Willing to do something about it?

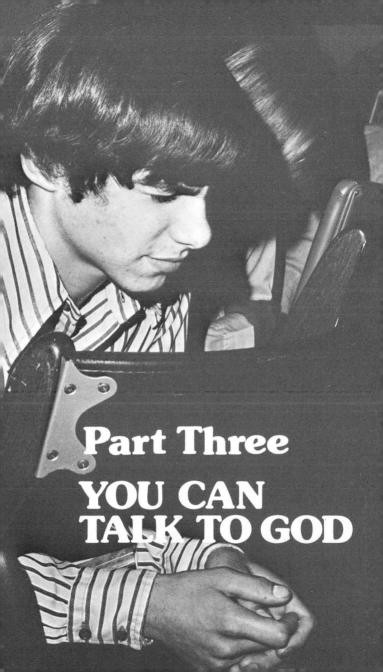

Part Three

YOU CAN TALK TO GOD

10

Do You Really Want To Pray?

In a fast-moving world of fast-moving everythings, perhaps it's foolish to expect anyone to slow down long enough to pray.

It does seem that not many kids spend much of their day in conversation with God. One of the reasons is that they don't know much about how to go about it. So, maybe it would be a good idea to spend a few short pages on this crucial subject.

Think with me for a few moments.

In your own life, what is prayer usually like?

Is it five minutes of "bless this and bless that," punctuated by yawns? Or is it more like two minutes beside the bed while your tired brain turns a couple slow revolutions before it finally dies for the night? Maybe you have occasionally reached the dizzying heights of spirituality by investing fifteen fervent moments interceding for a friend who is expected to attend a forthcoming evangelistic meeting. Or do you just pray when you are really in a jam? Panic prayers, we call them.

Could be you are among those millions who have told themselves repeatedly that you are "going to pray more from now on" but never actually do it.

Or might it possibly be that you are part of that bored bunch who dig folk singers, "gospel rock concerts," and other such crowd-infested excitements, but avoid *prayer meetings* like the bubonic plague?

Brother, you need help! You need to close in with God himself. You need to set up some sound communications with the Center of the universe. If you've let prayer lay unused on the fringe of your daily existence, you are missing the real pulse of Christianity.

Whatever your prayer condition might be, chances are if you have read the book this far, the following suggestions will be of some help.

HOW TO BEGIN

Pray According to Appetite

A long time ago I read about a man named Praying Hyde. I discovered that he had such an enormous appetite for God that he prayed for hours, and sometimes days, without intermission.

It sounded wonderful. I tried it. I failed miserably. Why? Because I was trying to pray *his* prayers without *his* appetite. I was not ready for so much so soon.

But then I found that praying as much as I *was* ready for gave me a growing appetite. At any given time in life we should be praying as much as we *ought*. If we pray as much as we ought, God will enlarge our desire for conversation with Him.

Pray According to Need

Most young people *worry* according to their need, but seldom *pray* according to their need. Think of it: You never worry less than necessary. You never complain less than you need to. If either worry or gripes brought answers from heaven, you would be nearly drowning in blessings.

The trouble is that so much sense of need which should be channeled up to God is loaded instead onto the useless merry-go-round of fretting and stewing. Spare your fingernails, and save on Roll-Aids . . . Pray!

Pray According to Scripture

There are three facts to be remembered in this connection:

1. The Bible tells us *the basis of our approach to God*. It is the sacrifice of Jesus on our behalf.

If God permits us into His presence, He does so only because the death of Jesus has given us legal access to His throne room. We cannot come to the Father simply because we need a heavenly handout. God receives us into His court of prayer only for His Son's sake. Every time we pray we must realize that we are heard for *His sake*, not ours.

2. The Bible also tells us *in what manner to approach God*.

To pray is to walk into a throne room. The King himself is presiding and must be approached according to His own regal regulations. Respect, humility, honesty, and gratitude are the stipulations.

3. The Bible tells us *how we may recieve things from God*.

This part of the subject is so deep and so vast that volumes cannot exhaust it, much less a few lines. But let's reduce it

as well as possible to the point of under-
standability. Notice the following conditions
which must be met in order to get answers
to prayer:

    a. All sins must be forgiven (Ps. 66:18).
    b. All requests must be in harmony with
       the will of God (1 John 5:14).
    c. All motives must be right. We must
       want something primarily for the pur-
       pose of making God, not ourselves,
       look better (James 4:3).
    d. All answers must be received by faith.
       Having requested, we must then place
       our confidence in God to perform what
       He promised (Mark 11:24).

HOW TO GET AT IT

Let's assume you are alone in a room,
or on a hillside, or anyplace else. You may
be standing, sitting, bent double, or in any
other position. The thing that matters is
that you want to talk to God. May I suggest
some down-to-earth matters which may be
of some help.

First of All, Pray Early If You Can

Never go to breakfast before going to
God. A great Scotsman once wrote, "I feel
it is far better to begin with God—to see
His face first, to get my soul near Him—

before it is near another." So I say, "Pray early," and the thing that comes to your mind is, "How do I get out of bed to do it?" My answer is very simple: "Get up!" Don't pray about getting up, just get up! If it seems impossible, then go to bed earlier the night before, and you will usually have your solution.

In the Next Place, Pray Alone

It is good to pray in the prayer meeting. It is better to pray in the family. But it is absolutely imperative to pray alone with God. Find a hideaway somewhere. Go to the attic or the cellar if you have to. Get out on a fire escape or under a porch or in the laundry room. But get away, and get alone at least once a day. And once you find that isolated spot try to get back there every time. There are fewer psychological adjustments to be made in a familiar place.

Third, Pray Awake

Many people find it very difficult to remain out of the warm embrace of both mattress and Morpheus. But there are strong measures which can be taken to lick sleep.

First of all, zap your face with cold water, so you can begin with an alert brain.

Take a shower, if necessary. Then, while you are praying, if you begin to feel drowsy, change your position at once. Walk around if you have to, or stand erect, or sit up straight. God does not care in the least what position you assume to keep on talking with Him. The important thing is that you do not lapse back into unnecessary sleep when you could profit by conversation with the One who made the whole world.

Fourth, Pray in Plain English

I suspect lots of people get hung up about prayer because they think it requires some sort of special vocabulary, like "thee," "thou," "thou art," and other such terms. If such words come *naturally* to you while you're praying, well and good. But don't bother with them otherwise. Talk to God in exactly the same words you use to talk to anybody else you really love.

A man who made a terrific impression upon me some time ago did so because he didn't sound like a tired preacher when he prayed. As a matter of fact, we were sitting across from each other one day, having some discussion. Suddenly I realized he was not even addressing me any longer. He was talking to God. He had changed the direction of his words so smoothly and unnoticably that I hadn't even noted just when he shifted gears. He talked to God precisely as he had been talking to me—honestly, and without any fancy words. It was great. You should do the same.

Finally, Pray in Good Company

Two things can be taken with you when you enter the important adventure of private prayer. One is a Bible. The other is a songbook. They are great companions. The first one gives you a chance to listen to what the Lord might want to say to you. The second is a great help to worship Him. You know, if you really care for someone, you like to say nice things to them. There have been an awful lot of people who have been very fond of God. And they have said a great many good things about Him in the form of songs and hymns. When you run out of ways to praise Him, these songwriters can come to your rescue. They have been at it longer than you have, and you will discover it is sheer delight to borrow some of their heartfelt phrases and use them to express your own worship of the Father, His marvelous Son, and His helpful Spirit.

WHY YOU SHOULD PRAY

I suspect I should have started this chapter at this point instead of where I did. It's a cinch that nobody will begin to talk to God without being first convinced that there are good reasons for doing so.

At any rate, if you are still with me, I'd like to give you three solid reasons for praying:

First, Pray Because You Need It

Now, that has to be the understatement of the century! You need it. Jesus himself obviously felt greatly in need of prayer during His quick trip through this mortal world. Well, if JESUS had to pray, then you and I are *desperately* in need of it!

This is no selfish motive. It's a sane motive. We eat to keep from dying. We pray to keep from dying. It's as simple as that. The church in the book of Acts prayed its *first* prayers for itself. They would have been blotted out if they had not. With dead religionists squeezing them from one side, and dirty pagans pushing them from the other, prayer was their only means of spiritual and physical survival.

You are under essentially the same pressure they were under. And the shoves are coming from the same sources. You can feel it from one of the two sides every day.

Secondly, Pray Because the World Needs It

Think for a moment. The Bible says God answers prayer. It also says that people do not become Christians unless someone prays effectively for them. If you get up some morning and pray for the eternal salvation of a friend and then find out later that he was saved, you have every Bible reason to believe he was saved *because* you prayed.

This being the case, you are forced to conclude that if you had *not* prayed, that lost one would have remained lost. To put it another way . . . your lack of prayer could contribute to his damnation.

If this is true, every time a Christian is not obedient in prayer, he is helping people to hell.

Now add this to the picture: The present population of the world is well over three billion. The vast majority are doomed. Unuttered prayers on earth can mean unutterable pains in hell.

Finally, Pray Because God Needs It

I would guess that this is the last incentive for prayer that we usually learn.

To accomplish the great rescue work which God has in mind for the creatures

He loves, He *must* have human cooperation. It is ingratitude of the worst sort to refuse to join Him in fulfilling His desire. This yearning of God cannot be satisfied unless He finds people who will work together with Him in prayer.

It is amazing that there are thousands of impressionable young fellows who feel enough affection for their football coaches to play themselves into insensibility for them, and yet those same young men feel virtually nothing about God's longing to reclaim a rebel race.

God will have many things to say to His followers before the judgment seat of Christ. But there are *some* things I doubt that He will ever say:

"You prayed too much."

"You prayed with too much feeling."

"You cried too much for the needs of others."

"You were too concerned with spending time with Me."

There is no doubt in my mind that one of the great passions of God is to find young people willing to appear 'abnormal' for the sake of praying and 'dull' for the sake of spending time alone with God.

Listen. If you *never* pass a tract, preach a sermon, or give a testimony . . . do at least *one* thing to justify your existence on this earth . . . PRAY!

Get up tomorrow morning and make a new beginning. PRAY.

Part Four

YOU CAN SERVE

11
Emergency!

A great ocean liner glided serenely through the cool black of the night. On board everything was peaceful and gay. Little knots of people gathered at favorite points here and there in the decks and lounges of the giant vessel. Conversation flowed freely. Comments were murmured concerning the beauty of the moon-drenched sea. Everything was normal. Everything was functioning as it should, and danger was neither in sight nor mind.

Suddenly, violently, the ship lurched. An awesome grinding sound vibrated along the length of the massive hull. Something had been struck!

Water began pouring in through a gaping wound of torn steel. The alarm shrieked. Lifejackets were hastily donned. Lifeboat crews lept into action.

Everything *normal* came to an immediate halt.

Nobody wasted valuable moments gazing at the moon. Quiet, harmless, pointless conversation stopped instantly. Shouts of fear and voices of command replaced it. Anyone who hindered the urgent job of saving lives was sternly forced aside at gunpoint. There was an emergency task to be performed in an emergency hour. Anyone insane enough not to conform to the needs of the moment was treated with appropriate harshness.

You live in a time of emergency—an emergency so enormous that words are not adequate to describe it.

There is no time to be ordinary. In the last analysis, there is not even time to be 'normal' in the sense in which that word is usually used.

A calamity has taken place. An immeasurable flood of sin has poured in on the human race. Men die daily with only the fires of hell ahead. Every twenty-four hours the population of the world increases by well over 100,000. If things keep going as they are now, the vast majority of those thousands will never hear one sensible word about how to be freed from guilt and acquainted with God.

If you were to divide the unevangelized nations equally among the missionaries now preaching the Gospel, you'd discover that each one would be responsible for the spiritual destiny of more than 50,000 individual personalities. What a staggering obligation is laid upon them! How can one frail mortal shepherd fifty-thousand safely through to heaven?

No wonder I insist on calling our present situation an emergency!

But the feature that makes the whole matter still worse is the fact that most Christians still insist on living 'normal' lives.

Only one type of Christian is suited to our age—the selfless kind. Had we been on that ship and refused to help lower lifeboats, we would have been no better than the rats in the hold. How much more heartless is the Christian who is preoccupied with attention-getting, emotion trips, crowd-conforming while all around him are kids who need God!

How dare anybody make plans to run his own little world—do his own thing—

while over half the globe has never even heard of Jesus!

There was once a man in England who could not bear being ordinary. He was a very successful fellow—a preacher, as a matter of fact. One day he was walking through the wrong end of London. He saw for the first time masses of society's cast-offs wallowing in gutters, bleary-eyed and bedraggled. Little kids with filthy faces. Mothers without husbands. Fathers without wives. People without houses. Houses that were not homes. Sin without restraints. And worst of all, lives without Christ. He could not tolerate success any longer. He abandoned his position among the ecclesiastical fat-cats and went as a messenger to the outcasts. His work spread round the world. It still goes on today. The man was General William Booth, founder of the Salvation Army.

Because one man refused to pamper himself, untold thousands have come to God.

How about you? Are you going to keep on being the usual blob?

12

You Can Witness

A very exciting discovery was once made by a group of young students in a Bible school. To their amazement they found that they *could* talk to people freely about Jesus! A lot of others were doing it. They had read reports about it. Heard rumors about successful witnessing. But it was all second-hand. *They* had never been free before.

They were a very ordinary lot with a fat supply of inexperience and fears. But God helped them, and they began to be broadcasters in a way they had never done before.

It all came about like this:

They were assigned to do some personal

evangelism one evening in a large metropolitan area. The next day many of them reported that they found it impossible, for various reasons, to get into conversation with strangers about spiritual things. As a result, some practical advice was given them, common experiences shared . . . and the following night everything was dramatically different.

These young people loved God and had long wanted to effectively testify. But apperently they needed down-to-earth counsel in order to know *how* to approach a lost sinner about Jesus.

There must be many Christians in the same spot these students occupied. So, this chapter is being written. If you find that you are one of them, then these paragraphs are just for you.

THE NECESSITY OF WITNESSING

One of the things that often clams kids up in indecision is a little sentence that the Enemy has been passing around for generations: "You can witness by your life and don't need to with your mouth." A careful look at that pious theory will quickly expose it for what it is. The Bible says, "It pleased God by the foolishness of *preaching* to save them that believe." Then how

in the world will anybody get saved through
folded hands and zippered lips? A holy
life can *prepare* a sinner, a prayer life
can *melt* a sinner, but only a *talker* can
convert a sinner. In short: Witnessing is
an absolute necessity. We'll get nowhere
until we are completely convinced on that
point.

THE POSSIBILITIES OF WITNESSING

Without a doubt more kids have come
to Jesus through the witness of other kids
in the past few years than by any other
means. The possibilities are almost un-
limited!

There is a bunch I know of right now
who travel around their whole region, from
town to town, every week of the year, for
the express purpose of sharing Christ. Do
they get any results? The last I heard,
young people's Bible classes have come
into being in at least three towns as a conse-
quence of their person-to-person talks in
streets, parks, and halls. So effective have
the efforts of these high school and college
youth been that the church with which they
work now has a regular teaching ministry
to about 250 people *outside* the regular
church crowd. Furthermore, they travel to
distant cities also. On one single week-end

excursion to a small city of fifteen thousand, they prayed with well over one hundred young people they met in outdoor encounters. Indeed, it is a rare night when they come home without having led several to Christ.

This story is typical of hundreds of similar ones across America. And *you* can be part of it!

AN APPROACH IN WITNESSING

Now we get to the heart of the subject, the hurdle that appears almost insurmountable to most—actually approaching someone and beginning a conversation about eternal matters.

But the hurdle is not nearly as high as it appears to be. And once the leap is made, you will wonder why you didn't attempt it long before.

Note some practical suggestions which will help you.

Obedience Precedes Grace

The first step is a matter of pure obedience. You will find that you do not get God's grace to talk to someone; but when you *do* talk to someone, you will get God's grace. You act first. Then God comes to your aid. You can count on Him every time. He will give you words to speak and guidance in how to speak them. But it's up to you to make the first move.

I recall riding across the Midwest on a train one day with a number of other passengers. I seemed to hear the Lord suggesting that I go and speak to a group of sailors at the opposite end of the car. I immediately stiffened with fear, and began to pray one of those panic-prayers that sheer fright has often squeezed out of me. I could think of several solid reasons why it would not be wise to make the trip from where I was to where I suspected I was supposed to be. God gave me no consolation whatever . . . and worst of all, He gave me no help. He just kept saying, "Go and speak to them."

I got up from my seat and pushed one foot ahead of the other. (They seemed to be as fearful as I was, judging by their inefficiency.) I went wobbling down the carpeted aisle in the direction of the men in blue. Still no help from on high. No burst of thrilling expectation. No heavenly revelations. No bubbly feelings in the pit of my stomach. Just pale face and plodding feet. Just as I approached the other end of the car, I chickened out completely and darted past them and onto the platform beyond. There I swallowed hard, took a lot of deep breaths, and felt no more spiritual than before. So I turned about, walked the few steps necessary, looked down at those rough-appearing guys and opened my mouth to tell them about Jesus. In that instant God came rushing to help!

When I finally obeyed, it was almost ridiculously simple. I had learned one more time that grace FOLLOWS obedience. I have had this lesson confirmed hundreds of times through the years. It is a basic principle in witnessing, and the sooner it is learned the better you will fare.

Love Prepares Hearts

Having insisted that the approach is up to you, I must add quickly that the *attitude* is also up to you. Go to unconverted fellows and girls with a genuine desire for their welfare. I don't mean a squishy emotional spasm of some sort, or a gushy sentimentality. Just honest concern. Such a frame of mind has always had an effect upon sinners. They find something almost unavoidable happening within themselves. They must acknowledge inside that you really care about them. The rottenest sinner recognizes love when he gets close to it. It may frighten him a little. He may not feel immediately grateful for it. But deep inside himself, under all the layers of cool and casual, or bold and belligerent, it has begun to pull down his defenses. Please understand: When a sinner feels his defenses falling, it does not mean he likes the idea and will immediately surrender to Christ. He may just smack you in the mouth to protect himself from self-exposure. Love never converts or convicts. The law of the Lord and the word of the gospel do that. But, love *does* break ground and do its part to get hearts ready for the plowshare of conviction. So love is indispensable.

Testimony Primes Interest

Ask to share with your listener something about what God has done for you. In spite of the upsurge of witnessing in our day, the fact still remains that the majority of Americans have yet to meet a testifying Christian face-to-face. It is still a novelty to most individuals. Which is one reason why it can be so helpful. It is a way of arousing interest without kindling resentment. Do not start by preaching. Begin by testifying.

Truth Pursues Consciences

If your testimony has awakened any degree of interest, you will often find yourself answering questions concerning what has happened to you. If no question is raised, it is well to ask the person you are speaking to, "May I show you the way of salvation from the Bible?" If he consents, take him at once to the pages of Scripture. If he is deeply convinced of his need, tell him what Jesus has done for him and how he must repent in order to receive the benefits of Jesus' death.

If, on the other hand, he seems to feel little guilt and still knows much gospel, you must go at once to the *law* of God so he will see his lostness as a lawbreaker.

Or, if he is not concerned about his sins and does *not* know the story of the gospel, then be certain to start with the subject of God's original plan and carefully explain why Christ had to die. When he has a good understanding of these two matters, *then* (and not until then) show him how he has broken God's laws and can look forward to nothing but punishment.

If you accurately declare the good news that Jesus died, and the grim news that sinners are lost, his conscience will be moved and God will be able to work inside him.

It is very obvious that this chapter only scratches the surface of the subject. Volumes have been written about it and still much more could be written. But if someone reading these paragraphs will be encouraged to launch out in a new venture for soul-winning, then these words will not have been written in vain.

Someone told me some years ago, "I've heard that when a lion gets his first taste of blood, he becomes an incurable hunter. I've found that witnessing is somewhat like that. Now that I have begun, I have an insatiable thirst for telling people about the Lord."

13

Joe Gets Guidance

As he walked home Joe realized that things were really beginning to pile up. The days had been going by far too fast and the time was getting short. As he turned the corner and started up Elm Street, the parade of fresh memories began marching through his mind.

It had all begun when that missionary had come to church one Sunday night about two years before. He had heard missionaries before, but this one impressed him like none of the others had. When he left the church that night he felt a sense of obligation which had never especially bothered him before. After he had become a

Christian, the circle of his interests had never moved out much farther than the edge of his own group of acquaintances.

But after that missionary talked . . .

But that was only the beginning. The next thing was the incident at the young people's meeting.

He thought he had completely forgotten about the missionary's visit, but when Herb stood up to give his testimony that night it all came rushing back. "I've been running around with the church gang for several years now," Herb had begun, "and I was mostly interested in living it up. But ever since that missionary guy was here a couple of months ago, my thinking has been slowly changing. I began getting bothered about the way I was blowing my time. And I got bothered more about the lost world he was talking about. Most important of all, God showed me somewhere along the line that I should be a missionary. Now I feel relaxed inside, and I'm starting Bible school in the fall."

Joe recalled that it seemed like most of the kids weren't particularly impressed by Herb's words. No one said anything about it afterwards, and he wondered if he hadn't let himself get too stirred up about the senior's commitment.

The next thing that came Joe's way began to make the whole business very complicated.

The big-time evangelist, Jim Dashee, had brought his team to town and they were having meetings at the auditorium. Instead of having their regular gathering at the church, the whole group piled into the bus and went downtown to attend. It was the third night of the campaign, and the big, breezy preacher was directing his message to Christians on the subject of "Guidance for Your Life." Somewhere in the midst of the message he said, "Take all your talents in one hand, your interests in the other, put the two together, and you will know the calling God desires for you."

That sounded very good to Joe. It was exactly what he had been waiting for! He sat right there in his seat and did just as Jim had said. Music, football, and college formed a nice satisfying pile in his imaginary hands. "This is it," his mind whispered eagerly. But on the way home he was "bothered" again inside. Somehow the rest that Herb had talked about was sadly lacking. There was only one thing to do—see the pastor.

"Sit down, Joe," the pastor said when Joe entered his study the following after-

noon. "How's the star halfback today?"
Joe mumbled something appropriate and
then laid his whole problem out before the
young minister. "Joe, it seems to me the
best thing I could do to help you is to turn
you to the Bible. But before I do that I'd
like to be very frank with you. It's been
clear to me for a long time that you have
a *double* problem. The first is what *you
want*. The second is what *other people have
been telling you*. Let's get at the first one
first. You *want* to go into music and college
football because that is where most of your
interests are. Am I right?" Joe nodded
assent. "All right, that's the first thing you
have to tackle," the pastor went on. "Are
you willing to push aside all of your own
desires and plans?"

Joe winced. He had been afraid of just
that. He swallowed hard and was about
to reply when the pastor continued, "The
whole point of being a Christian is to do
Jesus' will instead of our own. But the thing
that so often hinders us is that we build
up a wall of our own natural interests
—a wall so high that the perfect will of
God cannot get through to our minds."

That did make sense, Joe admitted, but
how about what Jim Dashee had said?

The pastor leaned closer. There was a

kind of pained look on his face. "There are lots of Jim Dashees going around the country telling people to be led by human nature instead of the Spirit of God. They all mean well, and as evangelists most of them *do* well. But somehow they seem to lack much light when it comes to the matter of Christian service. You were told something that night that simply is not true. It's been making God's will for you seem very complicated."

Joe shook his head. "It's complicated all right. Here I am, just about finished with high school, and I don't know what I'm going to do. I've always figured I'd go to college, get into athletics, and sort of . . . well, serve the Lord some way as I went along. But ever since that fellow from Africa spoke at the church, I've been thinking that maybe I've been on the wrong track. But, Pastor, I've gotta know one way or the other pretty soon!"

The preacher was back by his desk now writing out some references from the Bible. "You take these home with you, look them up one at a time and ask God for light. Then let me know how you come out."

Joe took the bit of paper, said good-bye, and started home. He turned up the sidewalk to his house. He paused long enough at the living room to greet his mother and then went quickly to his own bedroom. The books under his arm fell to the desk and a second later Joe dropped to his knees. He pulled the Bible over and began checking it with the little slip of paper. Matthew 26:29. He found the place easily. "And he went a little farther, and fell on his face and prayed, . . . not as I will, but *as thou wilt.*"

Nothing could have been more fitting, and Joe knew it. He'd read that verse many times, and yet it seemed new. Here was Jesus. His time, too, was short. And even *He* had to choose between His own desires and those of His Father. It went home to his heart and made him wilt inside.

How selfish he began to look to himself! How ridiculous his puny plans suddenly appeared!

Romans 8:14 was next on the sheet. "As many as are led by the *Spirit of God*, they are the sons of God." There it was again, the same thing the pastor had talked about. There was no denying it. The wishes of Joe simply had to be set aside so that the wishes of the Spirit could lead him. But one thing remained. "What does God want me to do?" He glanced down at the paper. Strangely enough there was only *one* verse left. He opened to the final chapter in the book of Mark. The words almost leaped from the page: "Go ye into all the world and preach the gospel to every creature."

It was some time later when Joe got up from his knees. The "little pile of plans" was gone from his hands, but *rest* was in his heart.

14

The Tragedy of Martha Speers

The story here told is substantially true. Names and places are altered, but the events took place as related.

It is very difficult to describe the house in which Martha Speers lived. Everything about it spoke of failure. I caught sight of it as I approached it on the narrow, dusty road which wound its way through the lush green Washington valley. I stepped out of my tired old Chevy and peered through the tangle which had once been the well-kept lawn of a modest pioneer house. Rambling through the disheveled grove were the remains of a fence. The wood was grey and rotted; the gate had sagged until it no longer swung. It yielded to my hand thurst with a distressing squeak, and I stepped through. Surrounding the frame building was the vestige of an apple orchard. The overripe fruit had fallen to the ground, and I heard it squash beneath my feet as I walked toward the back, looking for the door.

At the rear of the aged structure was a porch. Half the boards were missing from the floor, but the roof still managed to defy gravity, supported by two frail posts. There, clinging precariously to its rusted hinges, was the door. It was slightly ajar and from the opening there drifted the odors of stale food and stagnation. It was nauseating.

I called. From somewhere inside came the frightened reply, "Who's there?"

"It's Mr. Dugan, the new preacher," I said. I heard slow and faltering footsteps; the door eased open and she stood before me.

Her hair was grey, her face wrinkled, and her body bent. She was dressed in a faded denim jacket, heavy trousers, and high rubber boots. Her sad eyes were the windows opening inward to a mind which long before had begun to crumble under some unbearable weight. I found myself looking around at the interior of the room.

She saw my glances and began making pitiful little apologies about its unkempt condition. I tried to move the conversation over to something cheery, but even as I rambled on about an assortment of things, my eyes were irresistibly drawn to the incredible surroundings.

The room seemed little more than a mass of debris piled in a cave. The accumulation of generations of household goods lay in heaps. Through the center of the room was a crooked sort of path. At the far end of it was a stair leading to the second floor bedroom, and the opposite end terminated at the rear door through which I had just entered. We stood there on the "path," and she told me the whole dismal story of the building.

There were tears in her voice and a fluency that betrayed the fact that she had unraveled the same tale many times before. This very house had once been the bright and happy home of her parents and family. The father was a preacher of the gospel, and the home was the center of wise Christian training for all the children. But they had grown and gone their separate ways. Then Father and Mother died and Martha was left alone. From then on the whole homestead had gradually settled into ruin. That was the story of the house, a house that aged and decayed.

A few days later I heard the story of the woman who lived in this house.

Martha walked up the road one day to pay us a return visit. While we sat across from each other at the kitchen table, she pulled an old leather wallet from her bag and showed me the one picture it contained. I looked down at the cracked photo of a young boy as she began one of the most unforgettable stories I have ever heard.

When she was a young girl she knew Christ as her Savior. One day He had called her to be a missionary. The call was unmistakable, and she had every intention of heeding it. But then someone entered the picture—someone who was destined to turn her whole life into tragedy. He was a young and dashing doctor. He made glowing promises to the attractive young lady (others in the valley later told us that Martha was reputed to have been the most beautiful girl in the area). Martha was thoroughly enthralled, and they were married.

By then the first world war had come and her husband was swept away from her. He was in Europe with the American forces while Martha waited anxiously for his return. But he never came back to her. By the time he was discharged he had lost interest. Now and then she would hear reports about him but never did he return.

Appalled by the deception which had engulfed her, she clung desperately to the little son she had borne her wicked husband in his absence. She lavished upon that lad everything which a devoted heart could conceive. He grew to manhood and eventually went his way. Tragically, he bore the image of his father, not his mother. The only time he bothered to visit her was when her assistance check came. Then he would storm in, demand the lion's share, and go out and devour it in sin. The crowning blow came to Martha one day when someone reported to her, "Your son has been killed in a plane crash!" From that moment on she was overcome by insurmountable grief. It drained her body, emptied her soul, and eventually broke her mind. Hope died within her in that hour, and with it went all the meaning of life.

With tears in her glazed eyes, she returned the photo of her son to its place. There seemed to be nothing to say.

Martha was a failure.

Words could not undo her life.

Remembering brought only agony.

When her parents died, the house began to decay. When her *obedience* died, her life did the same.